This Book Belongs to

_____

First Edition May 2023

Published by Contatto Wellness Education Center
P.O. Box 6815
Myrtle Beach, SC 29572
www.contattowellness.com

My Trip to: _____

Dates: _____

Color the States you visited
(or the license plates you saw while traveling)

The License Plates I saw:

Most Colorful:

Most Patriotic:

Most Environmental:

Most Creative:

Most Wildlife Inspired:

Furthest from Home:

Most _____:

Most _____:

My Trip to: _____

Dates: _____

Color the States you visited
(or the license plates you saw while traveling)

The License Plates I saw:

Most Colorful:

Most Patriotic:

Most Environmental:

Most Creative:

Most Wildlife Inspired:

Furthest from Home:

Most _____:

Most _____:

My Trip to: _____

Dates: _____

Color the States you visited
(or the license plates you saw while traveling)

The License Plates I saw:

Most Colorful:

Most Patriotic:

Most Environmental:

Most Creative:

Most Wildlife Inspired:

Furthest from Home:

Most _____:

Most _____:

My Trip to: _____
Dates: _____

Color the States you visited
(or the license plates you saw while traveling)

The License Plates I saw:

Most Colorful:

Most Patriotic:

Most Environmental:

Most Creative:

Most Wildlife Inspired:

Furthest from Home:

Most _____:

Most _____:

My Trip to: _____

Dates: _____

Color the States you visited
(or the license plates you saw while traveling)

The License Plates I saw:

Most Colorful:

Most Patriotic:

Most Environmental:

Most Creative:

Most Wildlife Inspired:

Furthest from Home:

Most _____:

Most _____:

My Trip to: _____

Dates: _____

Color the States you visited
(or the license plates you saw while traveling)

The License Plates I saw:

Most Colorful:

Most Patriotic:

Most Environmental:

Most Creative:

Most Wildlife Inspired:

Furthest from Home:

Most _____:

Most _____:

My Trip to: _____

Dates: _____

Color the States you visited
(or the license plates you saw while traveling)

The License Plates I saw:

Most Colorful:

Most Patriotic:

Most Environmental:

Most Creative:

Most Wildlife Inspired:

Furthest from Home:

Most _____:

Most _____:

My Trip to: _____
Dates: _____

Color the States you visited
(or the license plates you saw while traveling)

The License Plates I saw:

Most Colorful:

Most Patriotic:

Most Environmental:

Most Creative:

Most Wildlife Inspired:

Furthest from Home:

Most _____:

Most _____:

My Trip to: _____

Dates: _____

Color the States you visited
(or the license plates you saw while traveling)

The License Plates I saw:

Most Colorful:

Most Patriotic:

Most Environmental:

Most Creative:

Most Wildlife Inspired:

Furthest from Home:

Most _____:

Most _____:

My Trip to: _____

Dates: _____

Color the States you visited
(or the license plates you saw while traveling)

The License Plates I saw:

Most Colorful:

Most Patriotic:

Most Environmental:

Most Creative:

Most Wildlife Inspired:

Furthest from Home:

Most _____:

Most _____:

My Trip to: _____

Dates: _____

Color the States you visited
(or the license plates you saw while traveling)

The License Plates I saw:

Most Colorful:

Most Patriotic:

Most Environmental:

Most Creative:

Most Wildlife Inspired:

Furthest from Home:

Most _____:

Most _____:

My Trip to: _____

Dates: _____

Color the States you visited
(or the license plates you saw while traveling)

The License Plates I saw:

Most Colorful:

Most Patriotic:

Most Environmental:

Most Creative:

Most Wildlife Inspired:

Furthest from Home:

Most _____:

Most _____:

My Trip to: _____

Dates: _____

Color the States you visited
(or the license plates you saw while traveling)

The License Plates I saw:

Most Colorful:

Most Patriotic:

Most Environmental:

Most Creative:

Most Wildlife Inspired:

Furthest from Home:

Most _____:

Most _____:

My Trip to: _____

Dates: _____

Color the States you visited
(or the license plates you saw while traveling)

The License Plates I saw:

Most Colorful:

Most Patriotic:

Most Environmental:

Most Creative:

Most Wildlife Inspired:

Furthest from Home:

Most _____:

Most _____:

My Trip to: _____
Dates: _____

Color the States you visited
(or the license plates you saw while traveling)

The License Plates I saw:

Most Colorful:

Most Patriotic:

Most Environmental:

Most Creative:

Most Wildlife Inspired:

Furthest from Home:

Most _____:

Most _____:

My Trip to: _____

Dates: _____

Color the States you visited
(or the license plates you saw while traveling)

The License Plates I saw:

Most Colorful:

Most Patriotic:

Most Environmental:

Most Creative:

Most Wildlife Inspired:

Furthest from Home:

Most _____:

Most _____:

Alabama

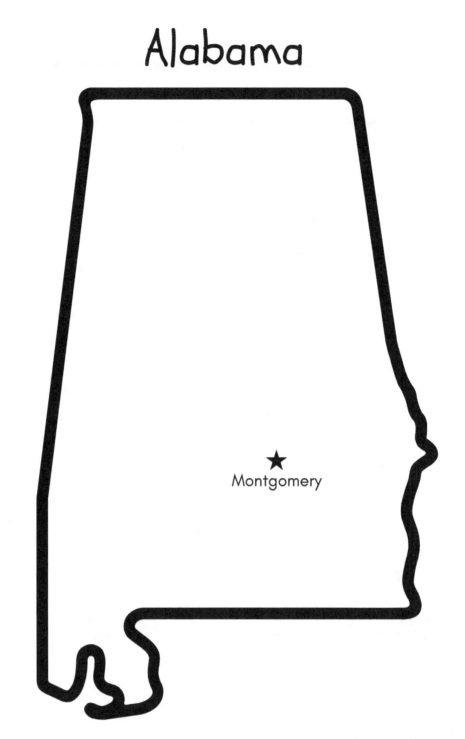

★
Montgomery

Huntsville is the home of the U.S. Space and Rocket Center as well as Space Camp. In Selma, the Edmund Pettus Bridge is the site of a landmark Civil Rights Movement event known as "Bloody Sunday," in which peaceful protesters were attacked by police. Mobile is one the busiest seaports in the U.S.

List where and when you saw a license plate from Alabama

_____

_____

_____

_____

_____

_____

_____

_____

Alaska

Juneau

Alaska has more coastline than the 48 continental states combined and all but seven countries. Alaska is the northernmost, westernmost, and easternmost state in the U.S. A good portion of northern Alaska is above the Arctic Circle, where the sun does not set around the Summer solstice, and does not rise around the winter solstice.

List where and when you saw a license plate from Alaska

_____

_____

_____

_____

_____

_____

_____

_____

Arizona

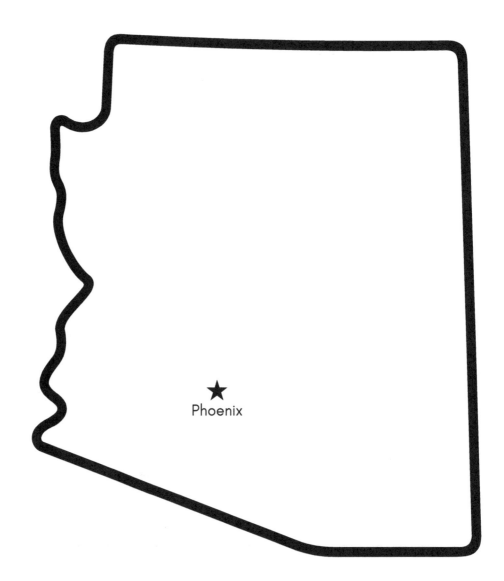

★
Phoenix

Route 66 goes through the north half of the state, passing through cities such as Flagstaff, and, as mentioned in The Eagles' song "Take it Easy," Winslow. The Grand Canyon is one of the Seven Wonders of the Natural World, and is over a mile deep at it's deepest point. Arizona is one of the states that create the Four Corners at it's northeast point.

List where and when you saw a license plate from Arizona

_____

_____

_____

_____

_____

_____

_____

_____

Arkansas

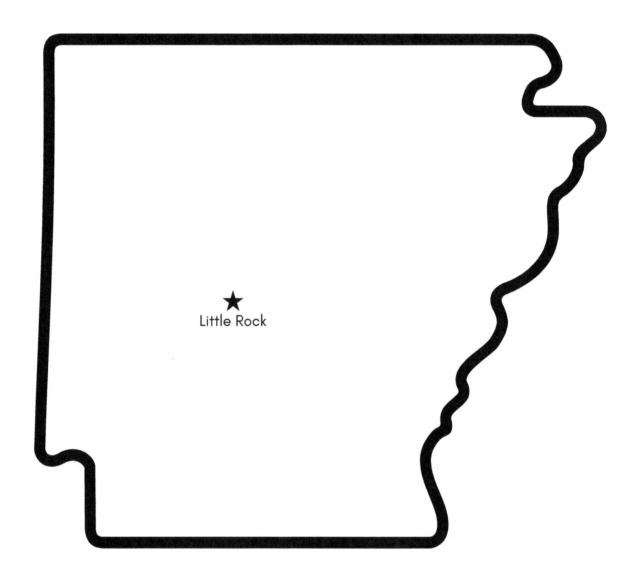

★
Little Rock

Toad Suck, Goobertown, Booger Hollow, and Greasy Corner are among the names of towns in Arkansas. Bill Clinton, the 42nd President of the U.S. is from Hope. Walmart is based in Bentonville. The S at the end of the state's name is silent because the name comes from an Algonquin Native American word for a local people.

List where and when you saw a license plate from Arkansas

_____

_____

_____

_____

_____

_____

_____

_____

California

Sacramento

Landmarks, stunning coastal landscapes, and natural wonders abound! Visit Golden Gate Bridge or Alcatraz in San Francisco, or go to the San Diego Zoo, Disneyland, or Hollywood in the southern half of the state. National parks like Yosemite, Sequoyah, Johsua Tree, and more are dotted throughout the state

List where and when you saw a license plate from California

_____

_____

_____

_____

_____

_____

_____

_____

Colorado

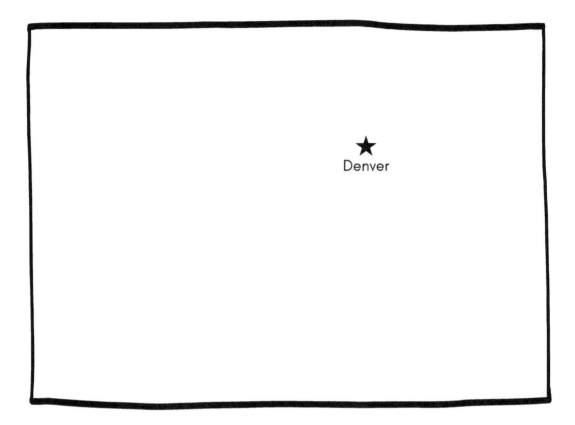

★
Denver

Colorado, known as the "Centennial State," is well-known for its majestic mountains, outdoor adventures, and interesting town names. From quirky places like No Name and Last Chance to picturesque towns like Telluride and Estes Park, Colorado captures the spirit of the Rocky Mountains. Denver, the capital city, offers an urban scene with a thriving arts culture. The state's natural wonders, including Rocky Mountain National Park and the scenic drives of the Million Dollar Highway, attract outdoor enthusiasts from around the world. Hiking in the summer gives way to skiing and snowboarding in the winter.

List where and when you saw a license plate from Colorado

_____

_____

_____

_____

_____

_____

_____

_____

Connecticut

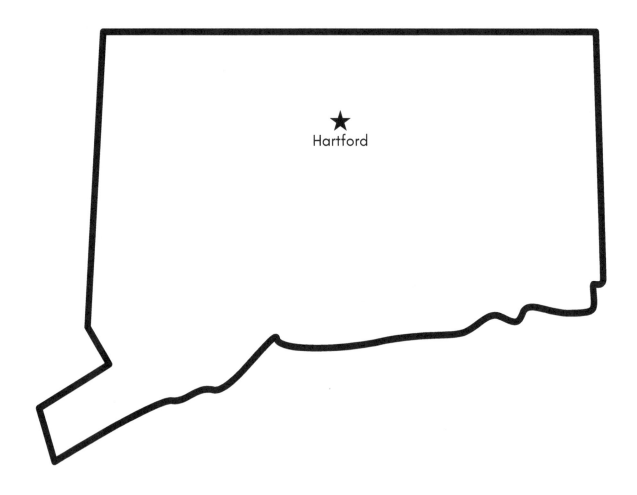

★
Hartford

Connecticut, nicknamed the "Constitution State," is a place where New England charm meets historical significance. From quaint towns like Mystic and Essex to unique place names such as Hazardville and Moodus, Connecticut showcases its own distinct character. Hartford, the capital city, is home to the iconic Mark Twain House and the Connecticut State Capitol. New Haven, known for its prestigious Yale University, offers a mix of cultural attractions and picturesque coastal beauty.

List where and when you saw a license plate from Connecticut

_____

_____

_____

_____

_____

_____

_____

_____

Delaware

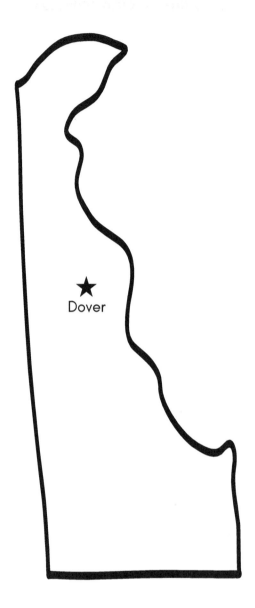

Dover

Delaware boasts a rich history and a charming blend of modernity and tradition. In the capital city of Dover, you'll discover the captivating Delaware State Capitol building, a symbol of the state's governance and legislative processes. Additionally, Delaware's beautiful coastline and beach towns, such as Rehoboth Beach, offer a magnificent escape for locals and visitors alike.

List where and when you saw a license plate from Delaware

_____

_____

_____

_____

_____

_____

_____

_____

District of Columbia

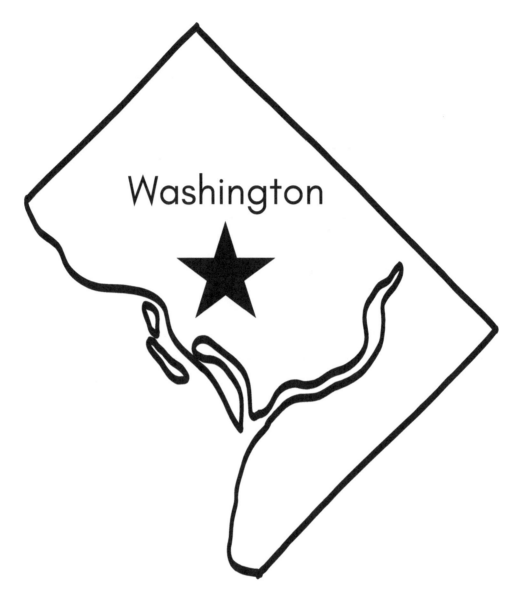

Washington

The District of Columbia, also known as Washington, D.C., is a unique federal district that serves as the capital of the United States. It is a city with a rich historical and political heritage. The district is home to iconic landmarks like the U.S. Capitol, the White House, and the National Mall, where visitors can explore museums and monuments that commemorate American history and culture.

List where and when you saw a license
plate from the District of Columbia

_____

_____

_____

_____

_____

_____

_____

_____

Florida

Orlando is home the world-famous Walt Disney World Resort, a magical destination that delights visitors of all ages. The city of Miami showcases a fusion of cultural influences and offers stunning beaches, vibrant nightlife, and the iconic Art Deco Historic District in South Beach. St. Augustine is the oldest continuously inhabited European Settlement in the U.S.

List where and when you saw a license plate from Florida

_____

_____

_____

_____

_____

_____

_____

_____

Georgia

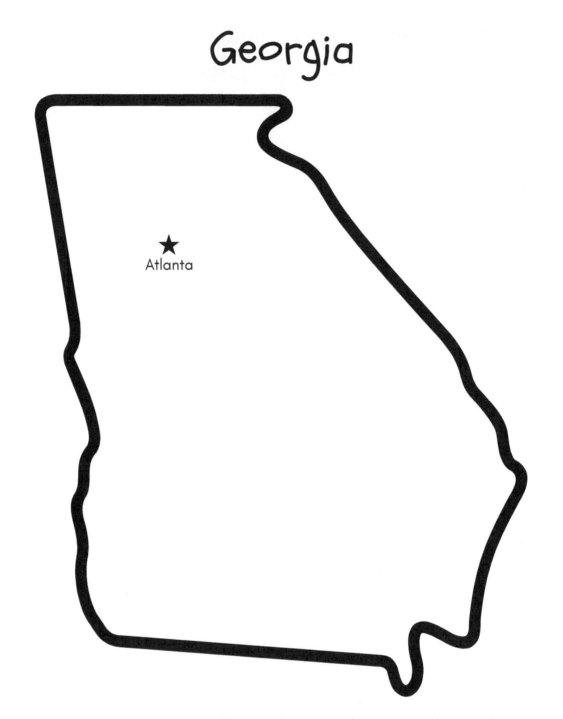

★
Atlanta

Georgia, the Peach State, offers a blend of historical significance and contemporary allure. Atlanta, the state's capital, features the Martin Luther King Jr. National Historic Site, a collection of landmarks honoring the civil rights leader. Also in Atlanta and surrounding areas, many movie studios have production facilities. Savannah, known for its well-preserved historic district and charming cobblestone streets, provides a glimpse into the state's rich colonial past.

List where and when you saw a license plate from Georgia

_____

_____

_____

_____

_____

_____

_____

_____

Hawai'i

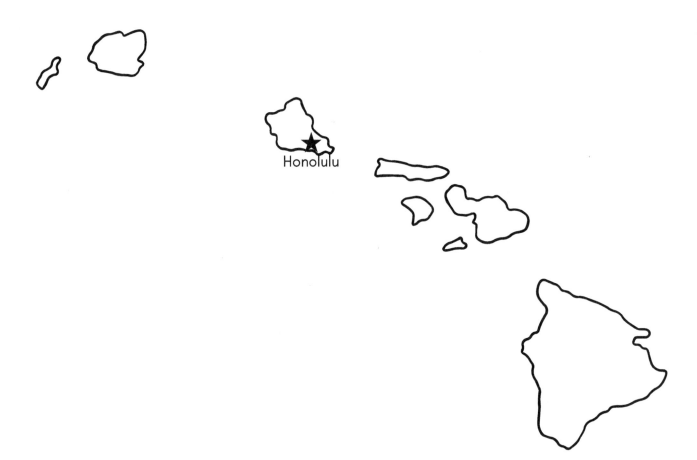

Honolulu

Honolulu, the capital city located on the island of Oahu, is home to the renowned Pearl Harbor National Memorial, which pays tribute to the events of December 7, 1941. The memorial stands as a testament to the bravery and sacrifice of those who served during World War II. Also on Oahu, hike Diamond Head for some of the most magnificent views you'll ever get. On Maui and Hawai'i, also known as the Big Island, explore volcanoes and surf some of the best waves in the world. Over 130 islands comprise the state.

List where and when you saw a license plate from Hawai'i

_____

_____

_____

_____

_____

_____

_____

_____

Idaho

★
Boise

Idaho, known as the "Gem State," offers stunning natural landscapes and outdoor adventures. Sun Valley is a world-class ski resort that attracts winter sports enthusiasts from around the globe. The rugged Sawtooth Mountains and the pristine lakes of Coeur d'Alene provide opportunities for hiking, fishing, and scenic drives.

List where and when you saw a license plate from Idaho

_____

_____

_____

_____

_____

_____

_____

_____

_____

Illinois

Springfield

Illinois, the "Prairie State," is a blend of urban sophistication and natural beauty. Chicago, the energetic metropolis situated on Lake Michigan, is famous for its stunning architecture, iconic skyline, and cultural institutions like the Art Institute of Chicago. The historic capital city of Springfield is home to the Abraham Lincoln Presidential Library and Museum, paying homage to the 16th U.S. president.

List where and when you saw a license plate from Illinois

Indiana

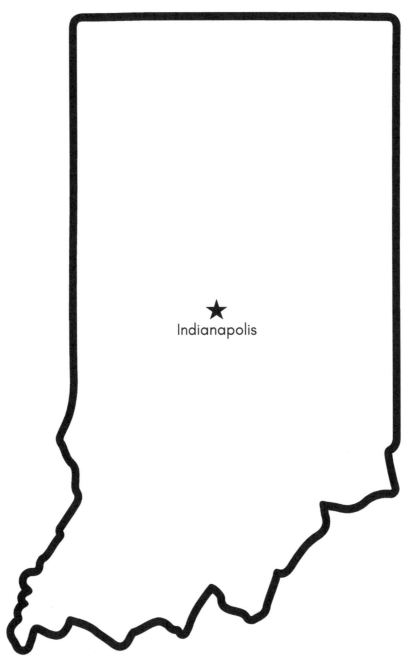

★
Indianapolis

Indianapolis, the capital city, is famed for the Indianapolis Motor Speedway, where the prestigious Indianapolis 500 race takes place. The charming town of Nashville in Brown County showcases a thriving arts scene and beautiful landscapes, particularly during the vivid fall foliage season.

List where and when you saw a license plate from Indiana

_____

_____

_____

_____

_____

_____

_____

_____

Iowa

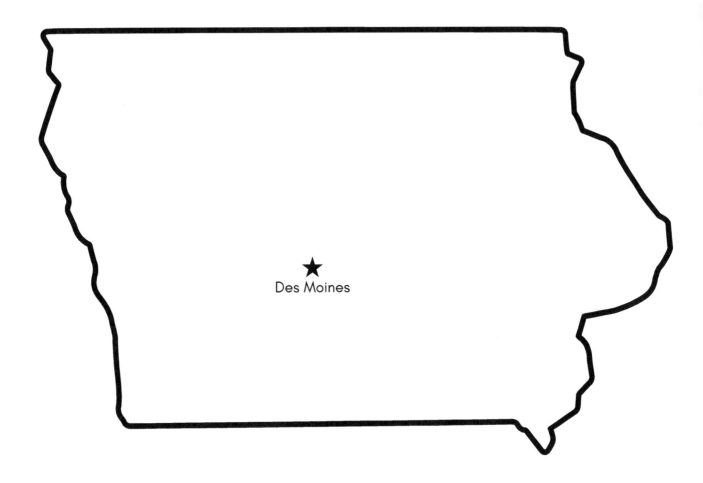

★
Des Moines

Iowa, known as the "Hawkeye State," is characterized by its vast farmlands and friendly communities. Des Moines, the state capital, features a lively downtown area, cultural festivals, and the Des Moines Art Center. The Field of Dreams movie site in Dyersville attracts visitors who want to experience the nostalgia of the classic film, including Major League Baseball games in 2021 and 2022.

List where and when you saw a license plate from Iowa

_____

_____

_____

_____

_____

_____

_____

_____

Kansas

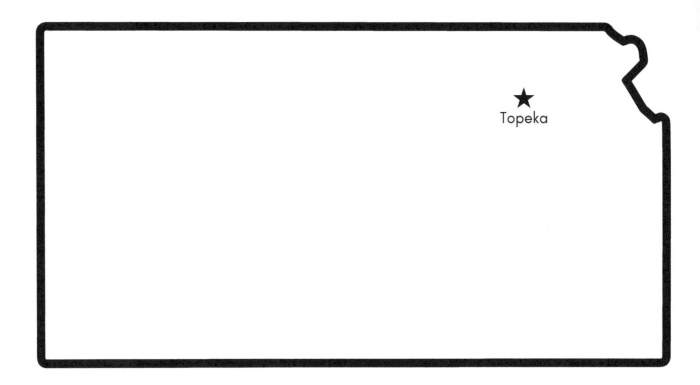

★
Topeka

Kansas, also known as the "Sunflower State," boasts a collection of towns with unique and intriguing names that reflect the state's charm. From quirky monikers like Toad Hollow, Mule Creek, and Skiddy to whimsical towns like Doodle Bug and Smolan, Kansas showcases its own distinct character. The state's capital, Topeka, offers cultural attractions such as the Kansas State Capitol and the Kansas Museum of History. Wichita, the largest city, is known for its aviation history and thriving arts scene.

List where and when you saw a license plate from Kansas

_____

_____

_____

_____

_____

_____

_____

_____

Kentucky

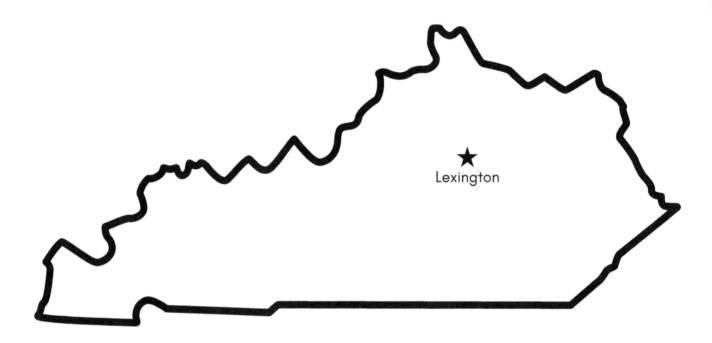

Lexington

Kentucky, called the "Bluegrass State," is famous for its rolling hills, horse farms, and country music influences. The state is home to towns with a touch of Southern charm and interesting names. From Rabbit Hash and Possum Trot to Monkey's Eyebrow and Fancy Farm, Kentucky's towns reflect its unique character. Louisville, the largest city, is renowned for the Kentucky Derby and its charming arts and culinary scenes. Lexington, known as the "Horse Capital of the World," showcases the state's equestrian traditions and beautiful thoroughbred farms.

List where and when you saw a license plate from Kentucky

_____

_____

_____

_____

_____

_____

_____

_____

Louisiana

★
Baton Rouge

Louisiana, the "Pelican State," is known for its vibrant culture, diverse landscapes, and its rich Cajun and Creole heritage. New Orleans, the state's largest city, is famous for its lively music scene, unique cuisine, and festivals like Mardi Gras. Baton Rouge, the capital city, offers a blend of historical landmarks, including the Louisiana State Capitol and the Old State Capitol.

List where and when you saw a license plate from Louisiana

_____

_____

_____

_____

_____

_____

_____

_____

Maine

Portland

Acadia National Park, situated on Mount Desert Island, offers breathtaking views, hiking trails, and diverse wildlife. The charming town of Portland showcases historic architecture and a bustling waterfront filled with seafood restaurants and shops. Rugged coastline, giant forests and quaint New England towns make up most of the northern and eastern-most state of the continental U.S. The only state that borders exactly one other.

List where and when you saw a license plate from Maine

_____

_____

_____

_____

_____

_____

_____

_____

_____

Maryland

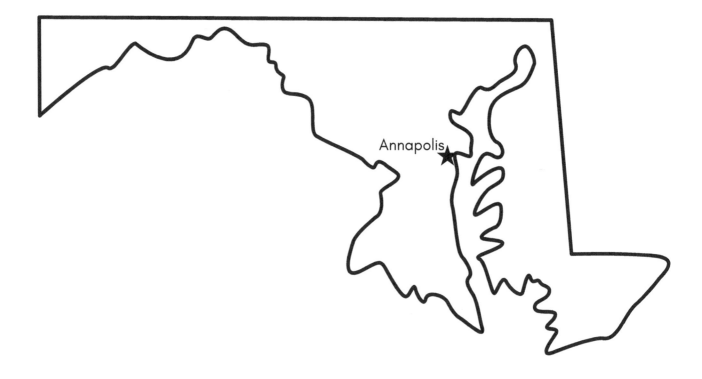

Maryland, a state with a rich colonial heritage, offers a blend of historical landmarks and modern attractions. In Annapolis, you can explore the United States Naval Academy and stroll along the streets of the Historic District. Baltimore, known for its iconic Inner Harbor, is home to the National Aquarium, showcasing fascinating marine life from around the world. Oriole Park at Camden Yards, home of MLB's Baltimore Orioles and opened in 1992, started a trend of building unique, baseball-specific stadiums that take local landmarks and the surrounding cityscape and incorporate them into the design of the stadium.

List where and when you saw a license plate from Maryland

_____

_____

_____

_____

_____

_____

_____

_____

Massachusetts

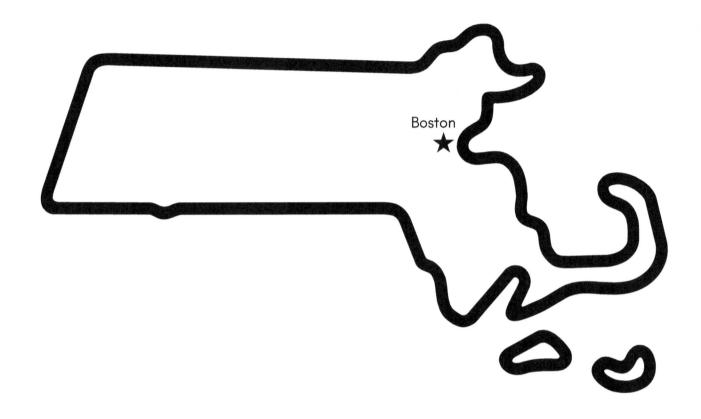

Massachusetts, the "Bay State," played a significant role in American history. In Boston, the state capital, you can walk the Freedom Trail and visit sites such as the Massachusetts State House and the Paul Revere House, as well as Faneuil Hall, the "Cradle of Liberty." Cape Cod, a popular summer destination, offers beautiful beaches, charming towns, and delicious seafood. In Springfield, you can visit the Naismith Memorial National Basketball Hall of Fame. In the western part of the state, visit the Berkshire Mountains and the renowned Tanglewood Music Festival, summer home of the Boston Symphony Orchestra.

List where and when you saw a license plate from Massachusetts

_____

_____

_____

_____

_____

_____

_____

_____

Michigan

★
Lansing

Michigan is called the Great Lakes State as it borders four of the five Great Lakes. Detroit, the auto-manufacturing capital of the world, also showcases a thriving music scene, distinguished art institutions, and the Henry Ford Museum, which celebrates innovation and American history. The stunning landscapes of the Upper Peninsula, including Pictured Rocks National Lakeshore and Mackinac Island, provide opportunities for outdoor adventures and relaxation.

List where and when you saw a license plate from Michigan

_____

_____

_____

_____

_____

_____

_____

_____

Minnesota

★
St. Paul

Minnesota, the "Land of 10,000 Lakes," offers abundant natural beauty and a cozy Midwestern culture. The Twin Cities, Minneapolis and St. Paul, are hubs of arts, music, and culinary delights. The Mall of America, a massive shopping and entertainment complex is in Bloomington. The North Shore, along Lake Superior, offers scenic vistas, waterfalls, and hiking trails in places like Gooseberry Falls State Park.

List where and when you saw a license plate from Minnesota

_____

_____

_____

_____

_____

_____

_____

_____

Mississippi

★
Jackson

Known for its charming Southern hospitality and a rich heritage that reflects its pivotal role in American history. The capital city, Jackson, offers a blend of historical landmarks, including the Mississippi State Capitol and the Mississippi Civil Rights Museum, which chronicles the state's significant contributions to the Civil Rights Movement. The Mississippi Delta region, characterized by fertile farmlands and the winding Mississippi River, is considered the birthplace of blues music. Visitors can explore the Delta Blues Museum in Clarksdale and experience the soulful rhythms that have influenced music worldwide.

List where and when you saw a license plate from Mississippi

_____

_____

_____

_____

_____

_____

_____

_____

Misssouri

★
Jefferson City

The "Show-Me State" is home to diverse landscapes and lively cities. In St. Louis, you can visit the iconic Gateway Arch, symbolizing the westward expansion of the United States. Kansas City is known for its jazz music and mouthwatering barbecue. The state also boasts stunning natural attractions, including the Ozark Mountains and the scenic beauty of the Mark Twain National Forest.

List where and when you saw a license plate from Missouri

_____

_____

_____

_____

_____

_____

_____

_____

Montana

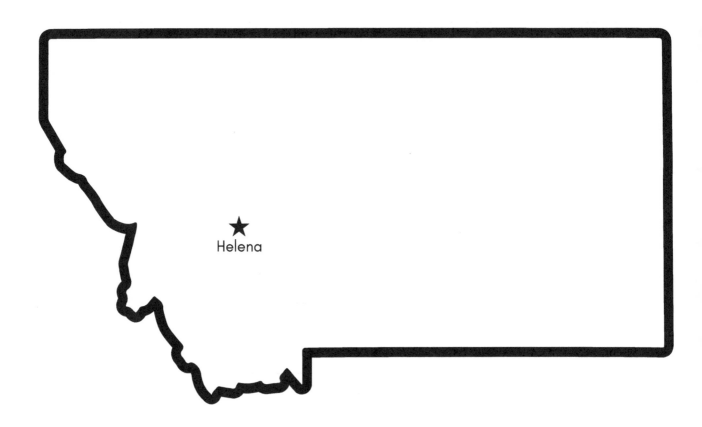

Helena

Montana, known as "Big Sky Country," offers vast open spaces, majestic mountains, and abundant outdoor recreational opportunities. Glacier National Park, located in the Rocky Mountains, features pristine lakes, glaciers, and diverse wildlife. Missoula is renowned for its arts and culture, while the historic mining town of Butte showcases its rich mining heritage. Montana is the fourth largest state by area.

List where and when you saw a license plate from Montana

_____

_____

_____

_____

_____

_____

_____

_____

Nebraska

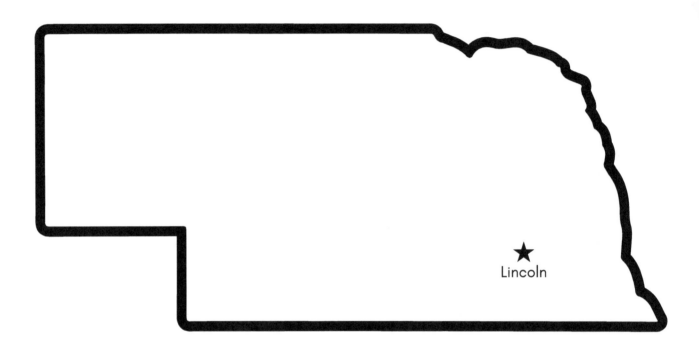

The Cornhusker State is home to towns with delightfully unique names. Frog Jump, Ong, Worms, and Magnet are just a few examples of the charmingly named communities found throughout the state. Omaha, the largest city in Nebraska, is esteemed for its arts scene, world-class zoo, and the historic Old Market district. The College World Series takes place annually in Omaha, and the University of Nebraska was home to the most dominant dynasty in college football in the 1990s, led by coach Tom Osborne.

List where and when you saw a license plate from Nebraska

_____

_____

_____

_____

_____

_____

_____

_____

Nevada

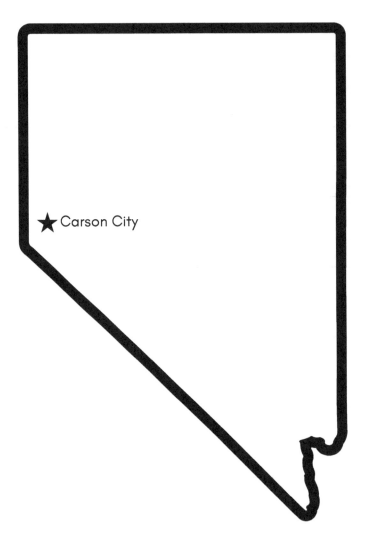

★ Carson City

The "Silver State," is famous for its dazzling entertainment and unique locales. Beatty, Lovelock, Jackpot, and Zephyr Cove are among the captivatingly named towns that contribute to Nevada's allure. Las Vegas, known for its non-stop nightlife, world-class resorts, and iconic casinos, is a global entertainment destination that never fails to impress. The capital of Carson City, sits just east of Lake Tahoe, a year-round destination for golfing, hiking, water sports, fishing, and all manner of winter sports.

List where and when you saw a license plate from Nevada

_____

_____

_____

_____

_____

_____

_____

_____

New Hampshire

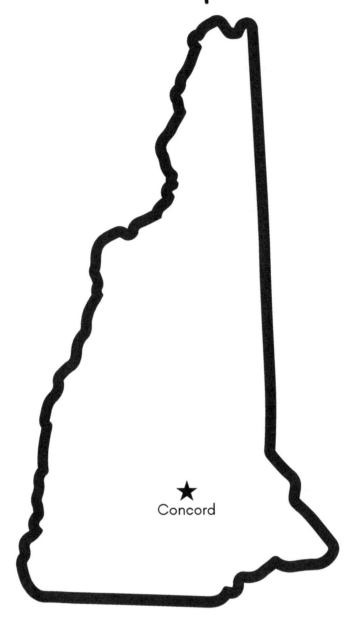

★
Concord

The Granite State offers a blend of natural beauty and small-town charm. In the White Mountains, outdoor enthusiasts can hike scenic trails and enjoy breathtaking vistas. The capital city of Concord showcases historical landmarks like the New Hampshire State House, while Portsmouth's charming waterfront and historic buildings provide a glimpse into the state's maritime heritage.

List where and when you saw a license plate from New Hampshire

_____

_____

_____

_____

_____

_____

_____

_____

New Jersey

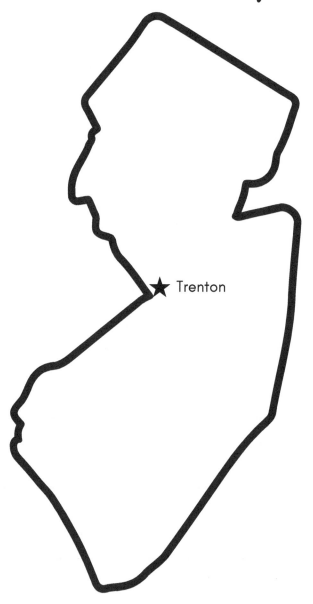

★ Trenton

The Garden State boasts a mix of beautiful beaches, bustling cities, and historic sites. Newark offers cultural attractions such as the Newark Museum and the New Jersey Performing Arts Center. Atlantic City, known for its lively boardwalk and renowned casino scene, attracts visitors seeking entertainment and seaside fun. New Jersey is also home to stunning natural areas like the Delaware Water Gap and the scenic Jersey Shore.

List where and when you saw a license plate from New Jersey

_____

_____

_____

_____

_____

_____

_____

_____

New Mexico

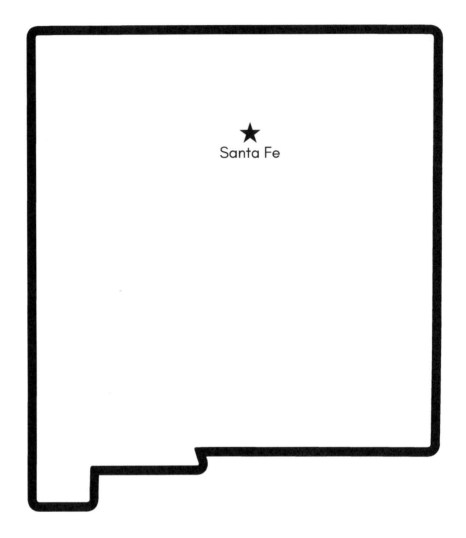

★
Santa Fe

The Land of Enchantment is a state rich in diverse cultures and natural wonders. Santa Fe, the capital city, is well known for its adobe architecture, dynamic arts scene, and the historic Plaza. Albuquerque showcases its Native American and Spanish heritage, particularly during the annual Albuquerque International Balloon Fiesta. New Mexico's landscapes range from the rugged beauty of the Sangre de Cristo Mountains to the otherworldly formations of White Sands National Park.

List where and when you saw a license plate from New Mexico

_____

_____

_____

_____

_____

_____

_____

_____

New York

Albany ★

The Empire State is a global center of culture, finance, and entertainment. New York City, the most populous city in the U.S., is a bustling metropolis known for iconic landmarks such as Times Square, Central Park, and the Statue of Liberty. The state also boasts natural wonders like Niagara Falls, the stunning Finger Lakes region, and the scenic Adirondack Mountains. From the relentless energy of Manhattan to the scenic beauty of Upstate New York, the state offers a wonderful array of experiences.

List where and when you saw a license plate from New York

_____

_____

_____

_____

_____

_____

_____

_____

North Carolina

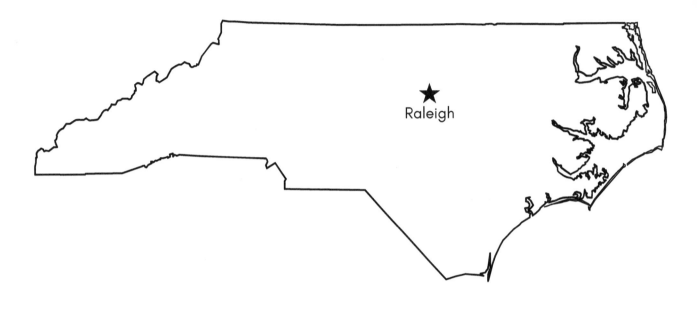

Raleigh

The Tar Heel State boasts a rich history and diverse landscapes.
Including Whynot, Toast, Bat Cave, and Lizard Lick, the state is dotted
with towns that evoke curiosity and a sense of whimsy. The city of
Charlotte stands as a bustling financial and cultural center, while the
scenic beauty of the Blue Ridge Mountains and the Outer Banks offer
breathtaking vistas and outdoor adventures, as well as historic sites
including the Wright Brothers National Memorial.

List where and when you saw a license plate from North Carolina

_____

_____

_____

_____

_____

_____

_____

_____

North Dakota

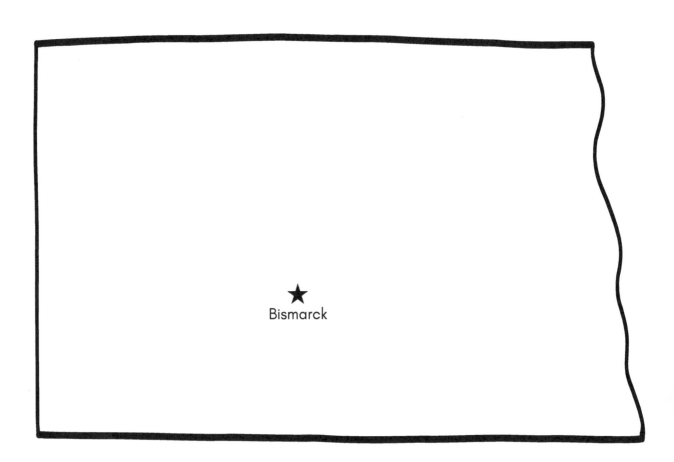

★
Bismarck

Amidst its vast prairies and open spaces, you'll find towns like Zap, Makoti, Buttzville, and Marmarth, each with its own intriguing story. The city of Fargo, with its impressive arts scene and friendly atmosphere, serves as a regional cultural hub, while Theodore Roosevelt National Park showcases the state's breathtaking Badlands.

List where and when you saw a license plate from North Dakota

_____

_____

_____

_____

_____

_____

_____

_____

Ohio

★
Columbus

The Buckeye State offers a mix of thriving cities and charming small towns. Columbus, the state capital, is a dynamic cultural hub with a rich arts scene and the acclaimed Columbus Zoo and Aquarium. Cleveland is home to the Rock and Roll Hall of Fame, while Cincinnati showcases its historic architecture and lively riverfront. Ohio is also known for its beautiful landscapes, including the picturesque Hocking Hills and the scenic shores of Lake Erie.

List where and when you saw a license plate from Ohio

_____

_____

_____

_____

_____

_____

_____

_____

Oklahoma

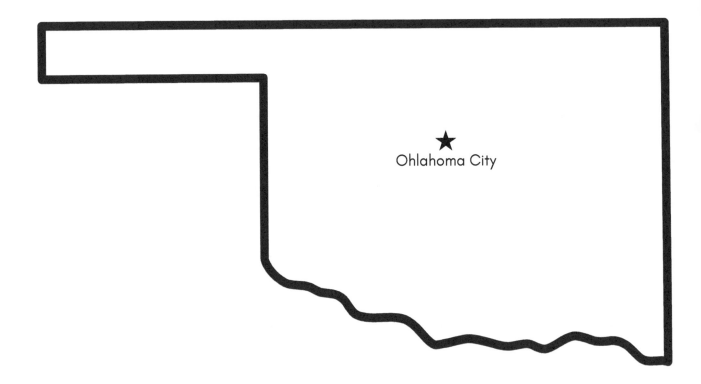

★
Ohlahoma City

The Sooner State is characterized by its diverse landscapes and rich Native American heritage. Oklahoma City, the state capital, boasts the lively Bricktown entertainment district and the National Cowboy & Western Heritage Museum. Tulsa showcases stunning Art Deco architecture and a thriving arts and music scene. The state is also known for its beautiful prairies, mesas, and the iconic Wichita Mountains Wildlife Refuge.

List where and when you saw a license plate from Oklahoma

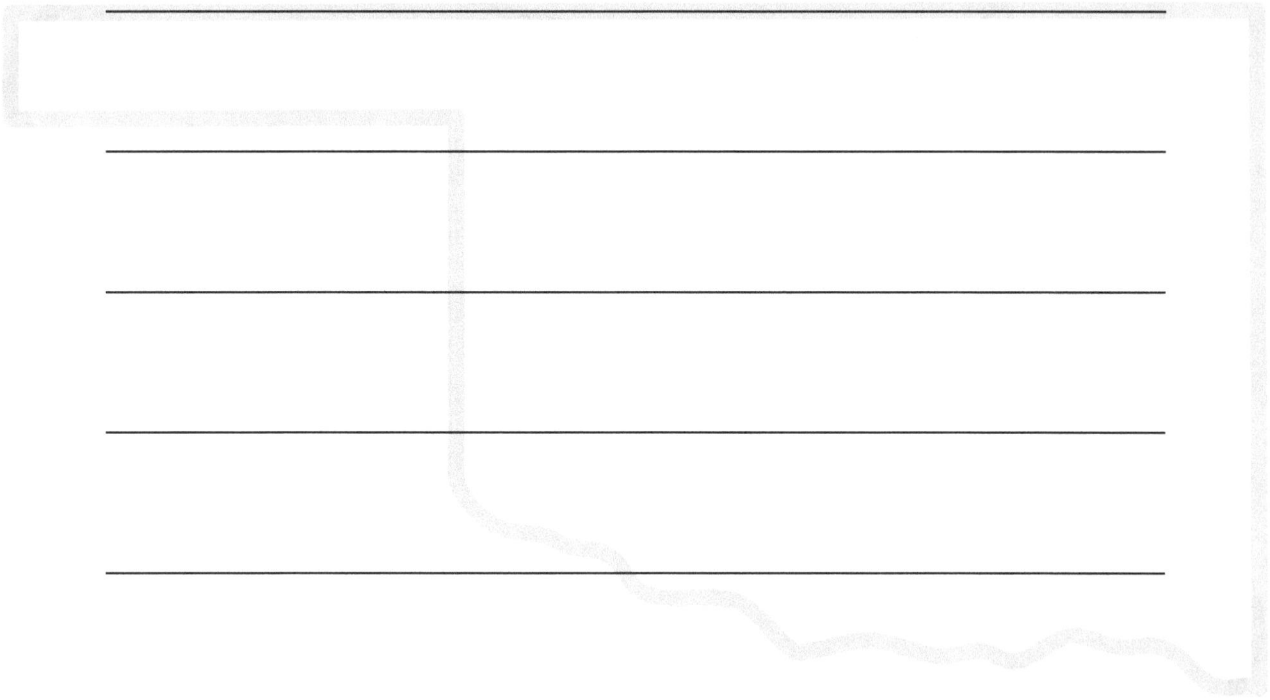

_____

_____

_____

_____

_____

_____

_____

_____

Oregon

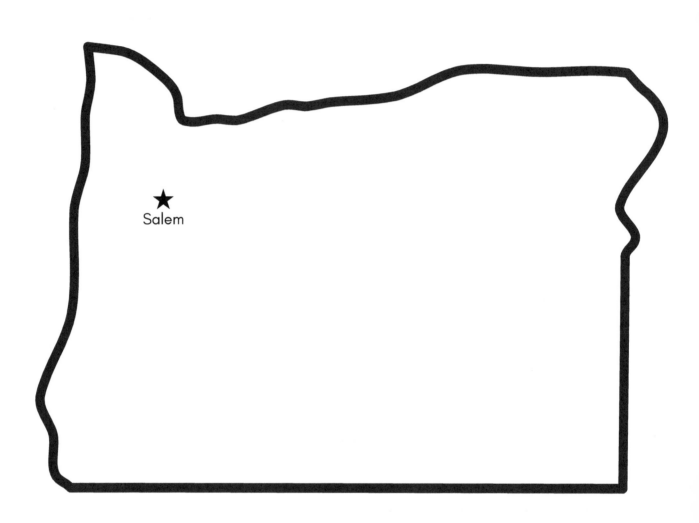

★
Salem

The Beaver State is a haven for nature enthusiasts and outdoor adventurers. Portland, the largest city in Oregon, offers a unique blend of hipster culture, craft food and beverage options, and picturesque gardens like the International Rose Test Garden. The state is renowned for its stunning coastline along the Pacific Ocean, the majestic peaks of the Cascade Range, and iconic natural wonders such as Crater Lake National Park and Multnomah Falls.

List where and when you saw a license plate from Oregon

_____

_____

_____

_____

_____

_____

_____

_____

_____

Pennsylvannia

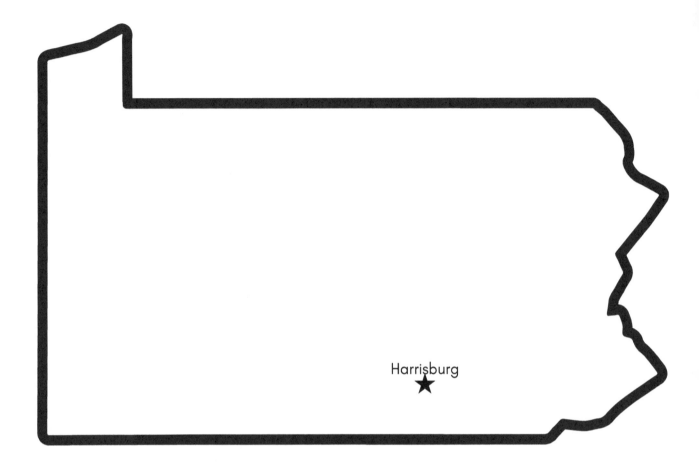

Harrisburg

The Keystone State is steeped in history and showcases a mix of modern cities and rural beauty. Philadelphia, the birthplace of American independence, offers iconic landmarks like Independence Hall and the Liberty Bell. Pittsburgh, known for its steel industry heritage, boasts a thriving arts scene and picturesque riverfront. The state is also home to charming Amish country, scenic state parks like Ricketts Glen, and the beautiful Pocono Mountains.

List where and when you saw a license plate from Pennsylvania

_____

_____

_____

_____

_____

_____

_____

_____

Rhode Island

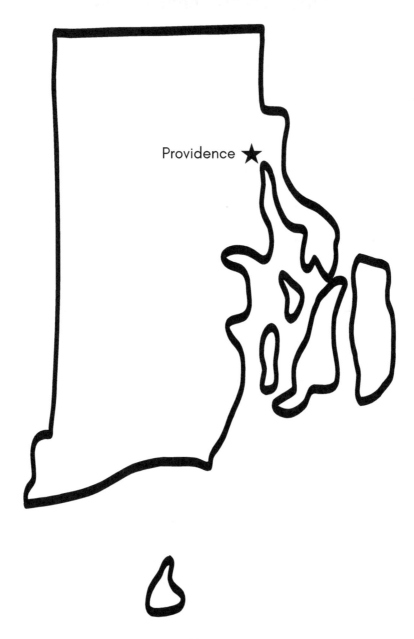

Providence ★

The Ocean State may be the smallest state in the U.S., but it is full of charm and coastal beauty. Providence, the capital city, is home to prestigious universities, historic architecture, and a compelling arts scene. Newport, known for its Gilded Age mansions and stunning waterfront, offers a glimpse into the state's opulent past. Rhode Island's scenic coastline, dotted with lighthouses and sandy beaches, attracts visitors in search of relaxation and seaside charm.

List where and when you saw a license plate from Rhode Island

_____

_____

_____

_____

_____

_____

_____

_____

South Carolina

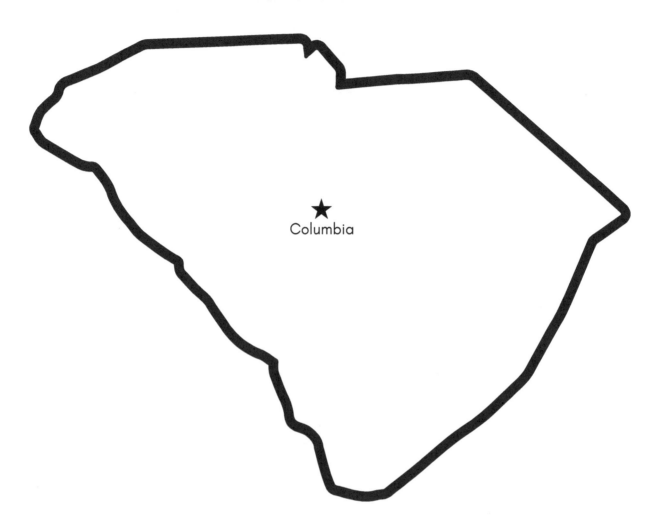

★
Columbia

The Palmetto State is home to towns with intriguing names that reflect its unique heritage. Cowpens, Due West, Ninety Six, and Yemassee are just a few examples of the charmingly named communities found throughout the state. Charleston, the largest city in South Carolina, boasts a rich history, stunning architecture, and beautiful coastal scenery. Congaree National Park is home to an incredible forest and astonishing biodiversity.

List where and when you saw a license plate from South Carolina

_____

_____

_____

_____

_____

_____

_____

South Dakota

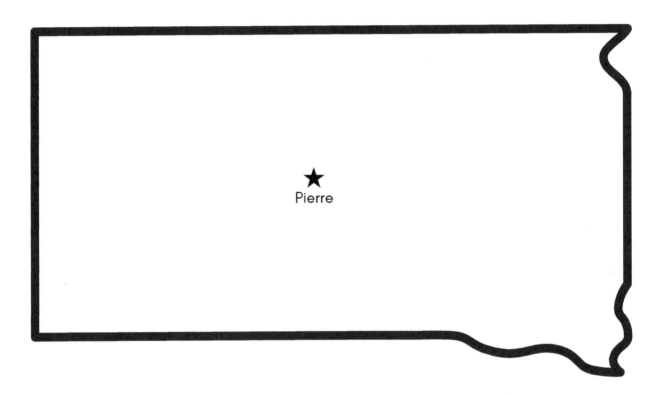

★
Pierre

The historic town of Deadwood is still an attraction for fans of the Old West. The iconic Mount Rushmore National Memorial, Crazy Horse Memorial, and the majestic Badlands National Park are among the must-visit attractions in the state. Sturgis hosts one of the largest motorcycle rallies in the world, annually drawing official attendance around 500,000.

List where and when you saw a license plate from South Dakota

_____

_____

_____

_____

_____

_____

_____

_____

Tennessee

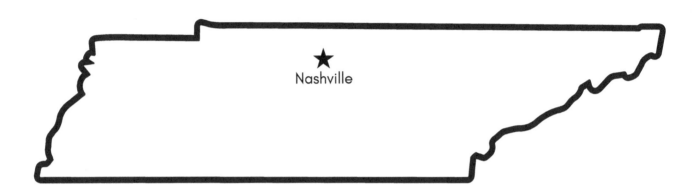

The Volunteer State is home to towns that embody its rich musical heritage. Nashville is the capital of country music, with numerous small venues where new talent and superstars alike could be performing any time you stop in. Memphis, known for its blues and rock 'n' roll roots, is where you can explore the iconic Sun Studio and visit Graceland, the home of Elvis Presley. Chattanooga is home to the Tennessee Aquarium as well as Lookout Mountain, the historic site of a crucial Civil War battle.

List where and when you saw a license plate from Tennessee

_____

_____

_____

_____

_____

_____

_____

_____

Texas

★
Austin

The Lone Star State is famous for its individuality amongst states. Texas was once its own Republic, and the state and many of its people still carry that rebel spirit. Houston, the largest city in Texas, offers a diverse cultural scene, while Austin, the state capital, is renowned for its influential live music and creative atmosphere. San Antonio and Dallas are important cultural and financial centers, respectively. Texas is the second largest state in both land area and population.

List where and when you saw a license plate from Texas

_____

_____

_____

_____

_____

_____

_____

_____

Utah

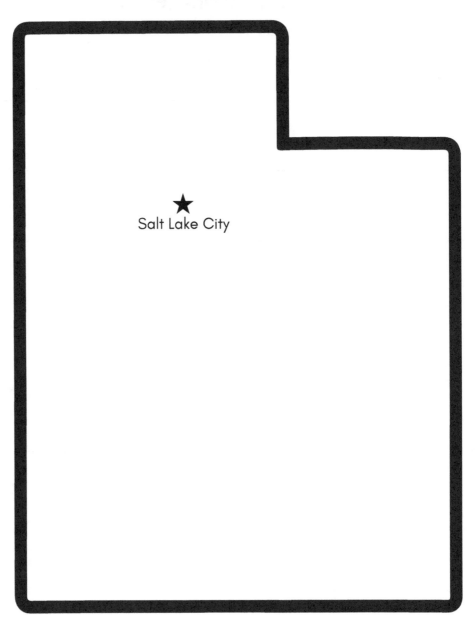

★
Salt Lake City

The Beehive State is characterized by its stunning natural landscapes and unique town names. From Blanding to Helper, and from Kanab to Moab, the state embraces its distinct western charm. Utah's iconic national parks, including Zion, Bryce Canyon, and Arches, showcase breathtaking rock formations, deep canyons, and otherworldly vistas.

List where and when you saw a license plate from Utah

_____

_____

_____

_____

_____

_____

_____

_____

Vermont

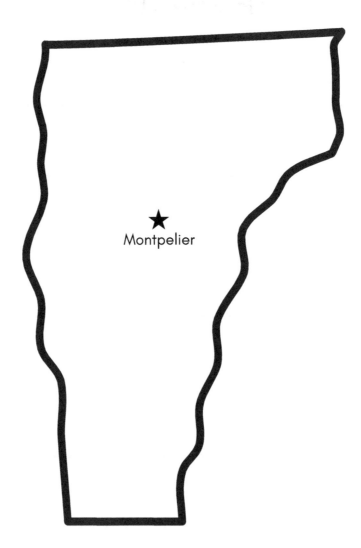

★
Montpelier

The Green Mountain State is characterized by its charming towns, scenic beauty, and a strong sense of community. Burlington, the largest city in Vermont, offers a wonderful arts and culture scene, while Stowe attracts visitors with its world-class ski resorts. The state's picturesque landscapes, such as the stunning fall foliage in the Green Mountains and the idyllic shores of Lake Champlain, provide a tranquil retreat for nature enthusiasts.

List where and when you saw a license plate from Vermont

_____

_____

_____

_____

_____

_____

_____

_____

Virginia

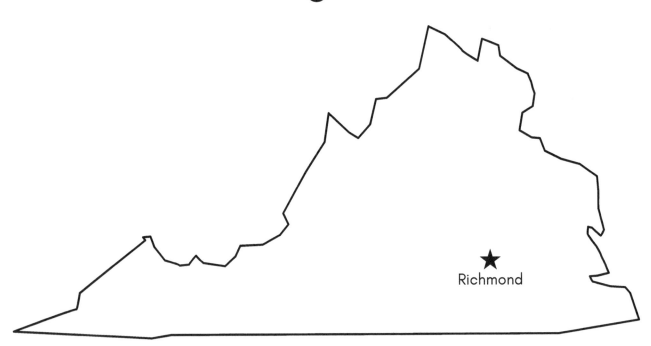

Richmond

The Old Dominion State is steeped in history and boasts a blend of natural beauty and modern attractions. Richmond, the capital city, showcases significant historical sites, including the Virginia State Capitol and the Museum of Fine Arts. The city of Williamsburg immerses visitors in colonial-era America, while Arlington National Cemetery in Northern Virginia pays tribute to fallen soldiers. The state is also blessed with natural wonders, including the scenic Blue Ridge Parkway and the iconic Natural Bridge.

List where and when you saw a license plate from Virginia

_____

_____

_____

_____

_____

_____

_____

_____

Washington

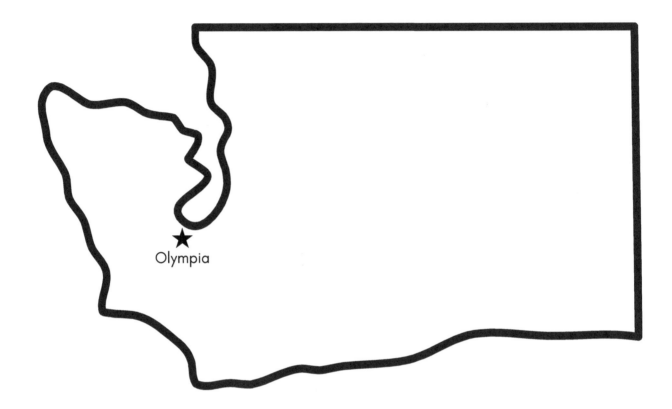

Olympia

The Evergreen State offers a mix of stunning natural beauty and energetic urban centers. Seattle, the largest city in Washington, is known for the iconic Space Needle, bustling Pike Place Market, and a thriving music scene. The state is blessed with diverse landscapes, including the majestic Olympic National Park, Mount Rainier, and the picturesque San Juan Islands, which provide opportunities for outdoor adventures and breathtaking views.

List where and when you saw a license plate from Washington

_____

_____

_____

_____

_____

_____

_____

_____

West Virginia

★
Charleston

The Mountain State is home to towns that blend natural beauty with Appalachian charm. Paw Paw, Lost City, Nitro, and Hurricane are among the communities found throughout the state. The New River Gorge, Harpers Ferry National Historical Park, and the stunning landscapes of the Monongahela National Forest are among West Virginia's notable attractions.

List where and when you saw a license plate from West Virginia

_____

_____

_____

_____

_____

_____

_____

_____

Wisconsin

★
Madison

The Badger State offers a mix of scenic beauty, modern cities, and hard to pronounce town names. From Minocqua to Sheboygan, Waukesha to Oconomowoc, the state's towns reflect its Native American roots. Milwaukee, the largest city in Wisconsin, is known for its brewing traditions and cultural festivals, while the natural wonders of Door County and the Apostle Islands offer picturesque getaways.

List where and when you saw a license plate from Wisconsin

_____

_____

_____

_____

_____

_____

_____

_____

_____

Wyoming

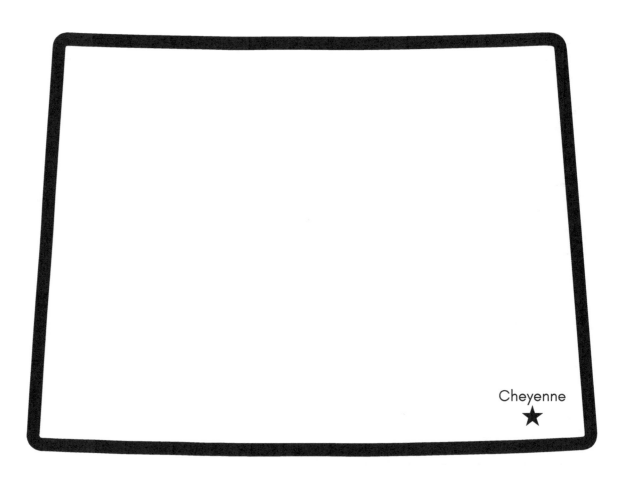

Cheyenne

Wyoming, known as the "Equality State," is known for its awe-inspiring landscapes and towns that evoke the spirit of the Wild West. Yellowstone National Park, Grand Teton National Park, and the dramatic beauty of the Devil's Tower are among Wyoming's iconic attractions. Hunting, fishing, and all manner of outdoor adventures are available throughout Wyoming.

List where and when you saw a license plate from Wyoming

_____

_____

_____

_____

_____

_____

_____

_____

Thanks for purchasing this book from Contatto Wellness Press! If you enjoyed this book, please leave 5-star review on the website where you purchased it!

Get updates on new titles and other exciting offers by joining our community!

We hope you had a great time with this activity book and that we'll see you again soon!

Made in United States
Troutdale, OR
11/04/2024

24420816R10071